Evangelism and Healing

Stephen Skinner
Vicar of St Mary's, Dalton-in-Furness
Adviser for Healing, Diocese of Carlisle

GROVE BOOKS LIMITED
BRAMCOTE NOTTINGHAM NG9 3DS

Contents

1. Introduction 3
2. A Breadth of Understanding to Healing 5
3. Emotional Healing: Healing the Whole Person 10
4. Healing our Bodies: Controversies of Physical Healing 14
5. Healing Relationships, Including in the Church 18
6. Healing in the Wider World: Expressing God's Healing 20
7. Practical Ways of Combining Healing and Evangelism 21
8. Conclusion 24

Acknowledgments

Thanks to the Carlisle Diocesan Healing Advisory Group, especially its previous Chairman, Bishop George Hacker, for their inspired thinking and sharing their experiences of healing, which have been an essential part of the development of both the ideas and suggestions set out in this booklet. Thanks also to my wife, Jane, who has discussed many of these ideas through with me, both before the script went into the computer, and in the various manuscript editions.

The Cover Illustration is by Ian Mountford

Copyright Stephen Skinner 1995

First Impression February 1995
ISSN 0953-4946
ISBN 1 85174 286 7

1
Introduction

Archdeacon Trevor Nash, in the 1991 'Henry Cooper Memorial Lecture' spoke about healing and evangelism as necessary partners in the full gospel. He says:
'Our mission to the people of this country will be impoverished and inadequate if healing and reconciliation are not part of our gospel for all mankind.'
He gives examples of where this partnership could be ministered and experienced in the church's ministry: healing of a malfunctioning marriage, preparation for death in a hospice through the sacraments, acceptance of disability through self- and God's acceptance and so forth. He believes that healing flows from faithful imitation of Christ, the wounded healer, into the wounds many have today.

I have had involvement in the healing ministry for all of my ordained ministry, and from my experience can fully concur with the views of Archdeacon Nash. In three separate parishes, and as Carlisle Diocesan Adviser for Healing over the last five years, I have been privileged to witness first hand an impressive variety of ways in which God has fulfilled his missionary purposes through the demonstration of his healing power. Most frequently it is thought that the healing ministry of the church is part of the *pastoral* armoury of the church. I have witnessed God bring healing into the lives of church members on countless occasions. But I also passionately believe that healing should be part of the *evangelistic* armoury of the church. A study of the gospels reveals that Jesus and the early church used God's healing power to affect those who were not within the community of faith. Their direct experience of God's healing became a significant factor in their healing. I have seen examples of this too, and will recount some later in this booklet.

Michael Buckley writes in the magazine *Healing and Wholeness*: 'Healing is the most powerful evangelistic tool in the armoury of committed Christians'.[1]

Through involvement in the healing ministry, I have been privileged to witness or hear of a variety of ways in which God has brought healing into people's lives. Where this has been in the lives of church members, it has unleashed a powerful evangelistic witness to others. In some instances the healing received (in a large variety of ways) has been of those who are not Christians, or church members.

An Example from Scripture

Let us consider briefly an example from Jesus' ministry. Perhaps the fullest account of a healing takes place in John 9, the story of the 'Man Born Blind'. He was pointed out to Jesus by the disciples as a living test case within the context of a theological disputation. The disciples accepted the common wisdom of the times, that disability was due to the effects of sin. In this case the only question was

---

1 *Healing and Wholeness*, October 1991 p 17.

whether God had punished the man because of his own or his parent's sin.

As usual, Jesus leaped over this sterile question, and proceeded to make an even more controversial statement in verse 3! In effect Jesus says, 'Forget past causal effect, look to the future, and what God can do for this man!' Jesus is preparing the ground for an impressive healing to demonstrate his compassion for this man as a real person beloved of God, not as a test case for theologians!

Jesus then makes a mud pack, and uses it as a sacrament—a physical conduit for the grace and power of God to flow into the man. The man obediently washes in the pool of Siloam and receives his healing—sight. The physical healing occurs first in this particular story, in other stories it comes after other forms of healing.

The incident might have rested there if it hadn't been for the Pharisees, who got upset because of the healing having occurred on the Sabbath. They proved themselves to be spiritually blind because they insisted that Jesus had to be a sinner to have worked even a miracle on a Sabbath. The man who could now see was unconcerned about their irritation, and grew in his belief that only a real prophet from God could have given him his sight. He is gradually gaining spiritual sight as the argument progresses with the Pharisees.

Finally, Jesus catches up with him, and seeks a straight answer from him about his beliefs. The man completes the healing process with a spiritual healing—by not only accepting Jesus as Son of Man, but worshipping him. It is a fascinating example of the interplay between physical and spiritual healing; this man receives both physical and spiritual sight. He ends the story *restored to wholeness*.

Conclusion

The works of the kingdom and the spoken word are like twin tracks upon which the gospel train can journey. These tracks can give direction, stability and authenticity to our message in the world. The partnership between these extends through our whole life, indeed through death and into the life-to-come. The works of the kingdom consist of various forms of healing which God brings about through prayer, as we shall see in chapter 2. Jesus' commissions to his disciples often include the 'dunamis' of preaching and healing; see Mark 16.15-18, Luke 9.2, and results in Luke 10. Morris Maddocks gives an excellent summary of the main thrust of Jesus' ministry, focussed upon healing. He writes: 'It is in the healing ministry of Jesus that we see the love of God incarnate, the Word made flesh, full of grace and truth'.[2]

It is my belief that although the healing power of Christ has continued to be at work throughout history, there is a special movement of God in these 'latter days'— a 'kairos moment' in which God is very powerfully at work. The great responsiveness of Christians throughout this country to healing celebration services testifies to the reality of encounter with God through healing prayer. Francis Macnutt writes: 'We are now seeing a return of the direct experience of God's healing power'.[3]

---

2   M Maddocks, *The Christian Healing Ministry* (London: SPCK, 1981) p 61.
3   F Macnutt, *Healing* (Notre Dame: Ave Maria, 1974).

2
A Breadth of Understanding to Healing

In Exodus 15.26 we read:
> 'The Lord said, "If you listen carefully to the voice of the Lord your God and do what is right in his eyes, if you pay attention to his commands and keep his decrees, I will not bring on you any of the diseases I brought on the Egyptians, for I am the Lord-who-heals-you."'

This important verse reveals to the Jews another name for God, that is: *'Jehovah Rapha'*. Thus we too learn that it is rooted in the very nature of God to heal. God pours forth his healing energies continually out into his creation. This is part of God's missionary activity. To be faithful to such a God we must invite people to receive this flow of God's healing grace into their lives. We must also help people experience this healing grace. Both these should be part of our mission.

An Illustration of Unity Within Diversity

God, the healer, desires to bring a whole range of healings into people's lives. Each is a means of reconciliation and restoration. It is my belief and experience that the process of growth into the image and likeness of God involves the synergistic working of a whole variety of different forms of healing brought by the living Christ through the power of the Holy Spirit. The power of this integration is well expressed by Jim Punton: 'Shalom speaks of a totally integrated life with health of body, heart, and spirit; attuned, open, in joy with God'.[4]

Perhaps the image of the prism can help us understand better the manner in which the different constituent parts of the healing activity of God, which is a missionary activity, relate together. The pure white light of the loving grace of God shines unceasingly upon our lives, and is refracted through Christ (as a prism) by the power of his Spirit into a number of different forms visible to our experience. At different times we receive Christ's Spirit as various forms of healing, corresponding to the different colours revealed through the action of the prism. In time, as we cooperate with God, and allow his gracious energy to come to us, we will receive healing in the ways described in general terms later. I will give brief descriptions here, and then expand upon the implications for mission in subsequent chapters.

How Do Other Writers Express This?

There are a number of other concepts used by those writing about this breadth of understanding to healing. Neil Cosslett writes of the need for *wholeness*:
> 'We must follow Christ's example and also preach and teach about the life of wholeness, life in all its fullness. So Christian healing ministry is much more

---
4 Reference unknown.

than bringing physical healing. It involves emotional stability, spiritual holiness and freedom from evil influences. The ultimate goal is *wholeness*.'[5]

David Dale writes of the need for *integration*. He contrasts the positive movement of our bodily, mental and spiritual facilities with the all too common experience in these days of disintegration. He writes:

'There is an intense longing for some form of personal integration by which the separate and disparate elements in human life and in society can be brought together into some kind of harmonious whole'.[6]

Other contemporary words which express our need for such a breadth of healing are: *harmony, poise, reconciliation*. Together they express people's greatest felt need for health and healing. As an essential part of the longing of the human spirit, they should, surely, at the same time be an intrinsic part of the Christian mission.

Healing of Our Spirits

Healing must be effected in our relationship with God. This is the most fundamental work of Christ, achieved through the cross and resurrection. These two events, central in human history, have great power for our healing and deliverance. In our evangelism we need to uncover and expound this healing power, which can heal our ruptured relationship with God. Leanne Payne writes:

'The first and primary healing out of which all other healing proceeds is the new birth. Once Christ abides within, one with our spirits, then his life can radiate throughout our souls—including our memories, willing, feeling, intuitive, and imaginative faculties. Then as his light encounters dark places of unforgiveness and woundedness within us, healing can occur.'[7]

This is the basic *spiritual* healing, and is the ground for all healing, for it is a prerequisite that we are receiving healing at the primary level of reconciliation with God in order to receive other forms of healing that God wishes to offer out of that restored relationship. Neither Jesus nor the early church engaged in healing for its own sake, but in order to give a context for proclaiming the lordship of Christ.

Healing of Our Emotions

This is often referred to as 'inner healing', but this can be a confusing term. This type of healing is primarily related to the work of God in bringing a new sense of shalom or inner harmony through the indwelling Christ. However, it should be distinguished from the renewal of the intellect about which Paul writes in Romans 12, for although our emotions and intellect are obviously related the processes upon which we concentrate when we are involved in 'renewing the mind' are different from those normally practised in this field of ministry. These processes include repentance, strengthening of the will, intellectual development. I thus prefer the phrase 'healing of the emotions' to that of 'inner healing'.

---

5   N Coslett, *His Healing Hands* (Basingstoke: Marshalls, 1985) p 109.
6   D Dale, *In His Hands* (London: Daybreak, 1989) p 34.
7   L Payne, *Restoring the Christian Soul* (Eastbourne: Kingsway, 1992) p xiv.

Past and present experiences of life bring to many people emotional problems, bad memories and maladjustment. Through both in-depth prayer (perhaps with the 'laying on of hands') and Christian counsel it is possible for people to find release and face life with a new sense of freedom. Consider for example the story in Luke 7, of Jesus' anointing of a 'sinful woman' (verses 36 and following). She was responding to our Lord's acceptance of her and demonstrated in her actions as she received Jesus' forgiveness that she was being healed within her mind and spirit. It is a good example of the 'healing of emotions' part of Christ's compassionate missionary work in bringing wholeness to those he met.

Physical Healing

This is the area that traditionally is considered the main arena of Christian healing. The models that are most generally followed are those from Jesus and the early church described in Acts. Today we tend to think of the evangelistic methods of people like Reinhard Bonnke, Morris Cerullo, Don Double, who pray for the healing of the sick as an intrinsic part of their evangelistic strategy.

Healing in Relationships

The area of healing of relationships, both within our churches and outside, is easily overlooked. However, we know that the quality of our relationships with others is of supreme importance to us. Recent research into the effectiveness of evangelism has highlighted the importance of people coming into Christian faith through friendship with Christians. God has created us to live in community. The building of such community is the story of the formation of Israel and the New Testament church, not so much despite but through many disagreements and subsequent healings of relationship. One of the key factors in this is *forgiveness*. Through the healing power of forgiveness deep disruptions in relationships can be dealt with, and the church give forth a witness of greater integrity to the world.

Healing in Our Communities and Society

As we continue to expand our understanding of healing, we move outwards towards consideration of the needs of our local communities and societies. It is clear that there is an enormous amount of dis-ease in our society today, we live in a society becoming sick through a whole range of different sinful behaviours and attitudes. The symptoms are only too obvious. To think of the gospel as offering a recipe or programme for restoring health to our communities is in my view a most helpful approach which could give the churches a radically different strategy for mission. Israel was offered by God a whole way of life which would enable their corporate life to be healthy.

Healing the Whole Creation

We can further expand our understanding of healing to embrace the whole of creation. The most visionary (prophetic and apocalyptic) passages in the Bible expand our notion of healing out into the whole of creation. Hans Kung has written that 'God's kingdom is creation healed'.[8] A passage which has had great influence within Scripture to generate this vision is Isaiah 65.17-25. St Paul in Romans 8.18-25 has a similar hope.[9] We further pursue this ultimate healing restoration of all creation in chapter 6. Kung's important statement lies in the context of his discussion about the significance to Jesus of his miracles, in inaugurating the kingdom of God. These healings have cosmic significance; they are 'the beginning of de-demonizing and demythologizing of man and the world and a liberation for true creatureliness and humanity.'[10] We are thus taught that healing is a prime agency for the mission of Christ and his church in 'rolling back' evil and furthering the kingdom of God—which is the goal of evangelisation.

Confirmation from Jesus' Teaching

All these forms of healing are part of the evangelistic mandate of the church because they form the intentional scope of the mission Christ undertook himself and set an example for us to follow. He worked not only physical healing, but a whole range of other forms of healing. He was concerned for the individual's material as well as spiritual salvation, as texts such as his 'manifesto' speech in Luke 4.18-19 demonstrate. Jesus did not of course engage in 'good works', in the sense of what is undertaken by contemporary charitable organisations; he was not a social worker. Rather his healing activity was of a much more direct nature. Whilst not decrying the good work of charitable endeavours, we do well to emulate Jesus' direct approach which got straight to the heart of people's needs.

In confirmation of this position Bishop Michael Turnbull has said:

'Evangelism without healing is neither a New Testament pattern nor credible in the modern world. Healing without evangelism has a hollow and sensational ring to it'.[11]

Is This Approach Too Broad?

I have been challenged about whether such a broad definition of healing is in danger of trying to expand healing to cover every aspect of the salvational activity of God (conveniently expanding my sphere of influence, also!). I would answer by saying that to express healing activity in this way need not so broaden our understanding of it as to render it vacuous, but rather it can add to its power and importance. This is much as one would argue for a breadth of scope to mission, in all its outworkings. One could argue analogously for a breadth of understanding to the concept of 'sacrament', beyond specific sacraments towards a sacramental understanding of God's grace-filled presence within his world.

---

8   H Kung, *On Being a Christian* (London: Fount, 1978) p 231.
9   See also Colossians 1.20.
10 H Kung, ibid, p 231.
11 From an Address at Burrswood Christian Healing Centre. Quoted on p 7 of a course introducing the healing ministry (AMCL) produced by the Acorn Healing Trust (Whitehill Chase, High Street, Borden, Hants. GU35 9QH).

A BREADTH OF UNDERSTANDING

An Expanded Definition of the Gospel

Healing in all its breadth is at the 'cutting edge' of the redemptive activity of our missionary God. The basic mission of the church is to proclaim this ongoing healing activity of God, and inspire people to align themselves with it through the leading of the Holy Spirit.

We could in fact recast the gospel's 'good news' in terms of *healing* —a highly attractive mode of expression for late twentieth century people. We have great need for the forms of healing stated above and often seek it in other religions or quasi-religious practices, having failed to find it in the church. Let me then offer this definition of the Christian gospel, and how the church can minister it:

'The Good News that Jesus came to both proclaim and embody is that through faith in him we might in God's good time receive healing; physically, mentally and spiritually. This belief is to be both proclaimed and ministered in humble service by God's people to all of his creation.'

An Illustration

I first observed a holistic approach to healing in a mission context at St Philip & St James, Walderslade, Chatham, where I was curate. The church used a many-faceted approach, developed over many years, composed of the following:

1. *Expository and evangelistic preaching had high priority.* The preaching of God's word was followed through immediately from the pulpit in prayer, relating the sermon to areas of need for healing, especially in terms of people's relationship with God.
2. *Membership of home groups had high priority.* Every church member was urged to join a suitable group, and within the close relationships possible many groups offered up healing prayer for people's relational or emotional needs.
3. *There were weekly opportunities for healing prayer within both Holy Communion and Morning and Evening Prayer.* A healing prayer team was available for this, and in addition members of the congregation often prayed for each other in the context of the continuing worship. We saw physical, emotional and relationship healing in these times.
4. *We employed a church/community worker with a trained team of Christian carers.* This ministry led to many instances of healing of mind, body and spirit. In addition this allowed God's healing to be taken out into the community beyond the church. Healing entered 'front line evangelism' as people were prayed for in their own homes, perhaps in the context of counselling or practical help.
5. *Deliverance ministry was exercised.* This was of course practised with care, within Rochester Diocesan guidelines. But we saw some dramatic long-term healing from the influence of the demonic, in the lives of both church members and the unchurched. These ministries were exercised for both pastoral and evangelistic purposes—a most effective alliance in what we can term a thoroughly holistic approach to evangelism.

3
Emotional Healing: Healing the Whole Person

I begin this section by setting out a number of different characteristics of this increasingly popular form of healing, also known as 'healing of the memories':
- The aim of such healing is to bring the healing touch of Christ to wounds inflicted in the past, so that the person might know increased wholeness in the present for the future. Leanne Payne writes:

  'To pray effectively for the healing of souls is to see the work of the cross (Christ's passion) made fully manifest in lives, and the gifts and fruits of the Holy Spirit flourish within the body of Christ. It is to see people come into maturity and wholeness and thereby the power to evangelize and to succour a world starving for love, truth and light.'[12]
- This form of healing deals with our emotional life which has been adversely affected by bad memories, effects of past sins, hurts inflicted upon us by others, addictions unresisted which now have strong psychological and physical grips. Healing of past hurts touches the damaged emotions and memories from all of life, going back even into the womb. Some teachers also believe that emotional healing might be required from sins committed by a person's ancestors (or curses placed upon them during or before their life).
- This healing may take place in a person's life when the Holy Spirit brings to the surface an unresolved issue, which has been suppressed, in order to bring an appropriate resolution by the power of the Spirit of Christ. Leanne Payne teaches that, as a person practices the presence of the crucified and risen Christ the deep symbols and images within the Christian tradition can 'resymbolise' the deepest symbols of the psyche so that a deep form of healing can be experienced.
- This healing is a healing of the whole person, especially of a negative psyche, damaged through sin or bad experience. The foundational pathway to obtain this inner healing is that of the sacrament of forgiveness, following repentance and renunciation of the past causes.

A national ecumenical organisation which adopts this kind of approach is known as *Wholeness through Christ*. Careful and thorough training is provided to those who feel called by God and their local church to become engaged in this ministry. The stated aim is that through Christ people 'find a new release from sins, bondages, fears and inner wounds that have crippled and often hindered their spiritual growth and development'.[13]

All this reveals that emotional healing is a very in depth approach to healing, taking someone as deeply into their past as they and the Holy Spirit desire. It

---

12 L Payne, Ibid, p xi.
13 The contact address is: Waggon Road, Brightons, Falkirk, FX2 OEL, Scotland.

allies together both prayer and counselling under the Spirit's guidance. Insofar as it enables the good news of Christ to be realised in people's lives, this is an aspect of the missionary endeavour of the church.

Glossary of Names
There are various commonly-used names for this 'healing of the whole person'. Each gives a different emphasis:
- *Healing of the Memories.* Such an approach has been pioneered by amongst others: Rita Bennett, Morton Kelsey, John Sandford, Ruth Stapleton, Matthew and Dennis Linn. The approach requires a prayerful, counselling atmosphere with either prearranged appointments or at least a fairly structured environment. The person in need is encouraged to reflect upon how their presenting problem or trauma might have been caused by past difficulties. The journey back in time might even take the client right back inside the womb (with full permission and great pastoral care). The person concerned is encouraged to relive their past experiences, doing so with Jesus present. Through prayer (which can be traumatic, and so requires maturity from those involved) the person is at best enabled to change the emotional power of the experience through the healing love of Christ's presence.
- *Prayer Ministry.* This approach is, in effect, pursued by many in the broad stream of the charismatic movement in their many large-scale meetings. For example, at John Wimber conferences people may receive prayer, which includes invoking more of God's Spirit as the Spirit does his sovereign work. Spiritual gifts such as 'words of knowledge' or prophecy are widely used to assist accuracy of prayer.
- *Healing the Family Tree.* This methodology has been particularly used by Dr Kenneth McCall. His books recount the success of a particular method of healing involving the laying out of a person's family tree. There follows an examination of any particular problems experienced by members of the tree, such as occult involvement, addictions, murder, rape, abortions. Prayer is offered up for these, generally with a Eucharist for the departed and client in need of prayer. McCall recounts many case studies where this appears to have worked.[14]
- *Sacrament of Confession.* This powerful means of healing has lain within the Catholic tradition for hundreds of years, and is now being advocated by those in other traditions. Matthew and Dennis Linn explain it well. With suitable preparation and through discernment of the underlying problem a formal (or possibly informal) confession of sin is made to Christ. In the receiving of forgiveness through the sacrament of absolution (possibly with the sprinkling of water) a deep healing is received. A new beginning can then be made. The Linns argue that such forgiveness received instils new life, 'pneuma', making us new creations.[15]

14 See K McCall, *Healing the Family Tree* (London: Sheldon, 1982).
15 See D and M Linn, *Healing of the Memories* (New York: Paulist, 1974). See also Grove Spirituality Booklet 50 *Personal Confession Reconsidered* by Mark Morton.

- *Inner Healing through Deliverance.* It is not the purpose of this booklet to enter into this still controversial topic, but mention must be made of the claims of inner healing through deliverance from evil, dark or demonic powers. The Linns also teach on this subject. Peter Horrobin of Ellel Grange and Glyndley Manor has written on this subject in great depth but also stirred up much controversy. The emphasis here is upon unearthing possible forms of oppression or possession which have harmed the person and, seeking direct deliverance, calling upon Jesus to deliver.[16]

There are many causes of dis-ease or hurt in our contemporary world, and the practice of these kinds of emotional healing can have good results. The meeting of these needs (fears, phobias, abuse, addictions, bereavement problems, occult influence) is a very real part of the mission of Christ's compassion, and this kind of pastoral approach can open up many evangelistic opportunities.

Summary

My argument is that our evangelism needs to have a contextualized depth to it so that these needs are addressed by the gospel message in a way that is actually dealing with the real problems faced. In my experience some people put over the gospel message in very superficial ways which fail to address these deeply felt needs. These needs are, without doubt, growing because of the stresses and increasing alienation of our modern world. Through using such an approach we can have a truly life-transforming message which contends with the pains of life in a more effective manner than other religions and philosophies. However, it is also possible to lean too far in the opposite direction of a 'needs-centred gospel' which focuses too much on the person rather than God.

In my experience as Carlisle Diocesan Healing Adviser, when we have held healing services the majority of those who have come forward have come because of their need for prayer for emotional healing. Even amongst church members of many years' standing, the pain that I experience with them of things that have happened to hurt their soul goes very deep. As evangelists we need to feel their pain and ensure we both share and minister a gospel that has depth to encounter it. These services have mainly helped regular church members, but we hope that as they experience healing they will witness about this to unchurched friends, and invite them for prayer.

Practical Suggestions

Here are some suggestions about how this can be done:
- Evangelistic preaching in which we minister to the depths of human pain, such as fear, loneliness, rejection, failure. This takes the evangelist well beyond basic prayers for people to 'invite Jesus into their life'. It means that effective evangelistic preaching will not only deal with doctrine and apologetics,

---

16 See P Horrobin, *Healing through Deliverance* (Chichester: Sovereign, 1991).Also Grove Pastoral Booklet 41 *Those Tiresome Intruders: Sharing Experience in the Ministry of Deliverance* by Graham Dow.

but also some of these life-needs where the depths of concern in people's lives are engaged. The word of God is released as a healing word. It is my experience that where I have risked touching these, people have listened very hard, and been touched at a deep level of their personality. It can require the preacher to reveal some of his or her own experience of healing; this can elicit a very powerful response at the level of people's emotions.
- Following up the preached word with substantial opportunity for people to prayerfully allow God to continue his work, rather than rushing quickly to the next part of the service. I term this 'ministering through' the word of God. In Dalton we allow time after the sermon for people to respond to the word, as God personally addresses them and touches their emotions through the power of his Spirit.
- Personal evangelism which is not afraid to invite people to seek God's healing love for dealing with past hurts, or other forms of emotional need. Integrating the message of Christ's love into such an approach as mentioned in this chapter is itself evangelism, as it encourages people to enter deeper relationship with our living Lord in every part of their being—emotions as well as minds and spirits.

In Autumn 1994 the churches of Dalton held a series of talks called 'Talking Points', open to everyone in the town. We aimed to engage with some of these inner concerns, so prevalent in our world. The subjects of loneliness, punishment, suffering, and family life were addressed by Christians with extensive experience of these topics, opening up the areas of potential need for healing before going on to describe how Christ could heal. These touched both Christians and those who were not Christians at a deep level of emotion.

4
Healing our Bodies:
Controversies of Physical Healing

There are a number of evangelists today who use healing as a central part of their methodology. Two of these with international reputations are Morris Cerullo and Reinhard Bonnke. It is generally fashionable for the media and much of the church to be highly critical of the techniques which they are employing. Reputedly they have had enormous success, especially in those parts of the world which are seeing rapid church growth, which we rejoice in. We must consider their strategy with care, and beware our own cultural tendencies towards rationalism and cynicism about the 'supernatural'. Most Christians claim to believe in God, but in effect have a 'deistic' concept which believes that God intervened in past times, but not today. Alternatively others believe that God affects the human spirit through his word, but is not expected to affect his world through any material means such as to bring healing, other than through some general good effect brought about through intercessionary prayer. But surely these positions are too weak for those holding to a God who not only created the world, but is still involved with it according to the 'incarnational principle' of involvement in its material as well as spiritual processes.

The Ministries of the Healing-Evangelists

What place do physical healings have within the evangelistic approach of Bonnke and Cerullo? According to their literature 'their' physical healings are held to be clear authentications of the validity of their call as ministers of the gospel. They act as huge crowd-pulling enticements to attend, with the strong prospect held out that anyone present can expect healing for themselves.

Their belief is that God wants to act into the lives of those who will have faith in his power to do miracles. They believe that they are especially anointed by God to act as conduits for his power. They stir the emotions of the crowds to which they speak, so that they reach the point of receiving the power of God's Spirit into their lives. As people receive the Spirit's power so they experience manifestations of God through spiritual gifts, high emotion, healings and deliverance. Their style of healing is focussed very much upon themselves as the primary channel for God, in contrast to certain other charismatic leaders such as John Wimber.

They claim to model their ministry upon the approach of Jesus, in preaching to large crowds and working miracles through his own faith in the Lord. But the following questions should be legitimately asked of their ministry:

- Should not greater weight be placed upon the role of other team members in also ministering healing, or indeed of the shared ministry of the whole body of Christ in this work? There is a perception of megalomania in the practice of this ministry which contrasts acutely with Jesus' servant style.
- Jesus worked the majority of his miracles not staged in front of large crowds, but 'on the road' and in the market places. He also tended to shy away from self-glory. Perhaps the big preachers should adopt a more self-effacing posture! The editor of the *Church of England Newspaper* is saddened that despite pleas from the evangelical constituency, Cerullo has not listened to various concerns they have expressed, and does not seem to want to work in openness and closeness with them.[17]
- The Christian gospel is about 'power in weakness', and about recognising human inadequacy and failure. Jesus experienced weakness and failure in his ministry; how much more will we in our ministry! Where then are the signs of this weakness, honestly admitted, in such ministries?
- The overall result of many of these campaigns is to encourage people to come to Christ for what they can get out of Jesus materially or physically. How will

17 *Church of England Newspaper* 19th August, 1994.

those such as Cerullo ensure the focus remains on Christ for God's *own* sake?
- There seems, in contrast to the position of this booklet, to be not a breadth but a narrowness of focus and expectation in the healing ministries of Bonnke, Cerullo and others. Where does relational healing in church and society enter into their preaching and ministry? Without it the danger is that people return into unhealed situations, and perhaps lose the healing they have been given.

Judgement Upon the Validity of Physical Healings

I believe that physical healings are certainly possible, and do occur within the context of both pastoral care and mission. They can be instruments and signs of the advancing kingdom of Christ. Such evidences of the present day activity of God need not in any way detract from the evangelistic message of the word, but rather add to it. I do not intend to enter debate on reasons why people are *not* healed after prayer. This has been well dealt with by Morris Maddocks in *Twenty Questions about Healing*.[18]

I would want to be very cautious of approaches to evangelism which focus upon the spectacular in the wrong way. They can encourage people to come to Christ for the wrong reasons, as a 'wonder worker'. Jesus avoided this temptation, and so must we. When healings come, by the grace of God, we can testify to them to aid faith, but not parade 'specimens' on stage, which actually often bring most glory to the healer. The same can be said here as of the 'Toronto Blessing'; it may be exciting for people to experience the power of God in their bodies (laughing, crying, shaking, fainting), but as John Wimber says:

'Most important to God are the fruits of that power encounter in a renewed prayer life, love of Christ, greater desire to witness, decision to lead a holier life'.[19]

Some reference needs to be made to the challenges made by Dr Peter May, who stands as an evangelical who has not yet been persuaded that any of the purported miracles of healing have actually taken place. He would quite rightly wish for every claim for healing by such as Morris Cerullo to be thoroughly investigated and proved true empirically. This controversy especially surfaced with the case of the 'healing' of Jennifer Rees Larcombe (a 'cause celebre'!).[20]

Principles for Assessing Claims of Healers

In this section I set out a number of broad principles to bear in mind when assessing whether a healing has indeed taken place in response to prayer. Clearly the evidence will always be interpreted differently by the various parties involved, according to their beliefs and interests. However I believe that some attempts should be made to assess any purported healing, whilst recognising the inherent difficulty of reaching any commonly agreed conclusion.

---

18 See M Maddocks, *Twenty Questions about Healing* (London: SPCK, 1988).
19 Quoted from a sermon delivered at the Free Trade Hall, Manchester in September 1994. For a detailed assessment see: G Chevreau, *Catch the Fire* (London: Marshalls, 1994).
20 The full story is in her autobiography, *Unexpected Healing* (London: Hodders, 1991).

1. We must get hold of as much medical evidence as possible of the condition of the patient before the healing occurred, preferably gained from more than one source and type of medical opinion. We recognise issues of confidentiality.
2. We must obtain an exact description of the illness, and what claim is being made for the 'healing'. Is it physical, emotional, spiritual? The diagnosis must be written down unambiguously.
3. We need plenty of evidence regarding the circumstances of the person's healing. We need details of how the healing was performed (methodology, manual techniques, prayers, counsel, emotional atmosphere, audience). We need information on the agents of healing, and their beliefs and practices.
4. We should know something of the patient's expectations at that time. Were they expecting healing, and of what sort? Was pressure brought to bear in any way (by friends, pastor, healer, audience…) and if so, what was its effect.
5. It is vital to obtain the fullest documented evidence of what healing took place at that time, and the course of subsequent events. What is the present state of the patient? Several medical opinions are required, including from those originally involved in the diagnosis.
6. We should look at motives, and the psychology of the one healed. It might be that emotional or psychological factors have been very important in the enabling of healing. We should assess also the spiritual repercussions. We can thus consider the whole psychosomatic effect.
7. The timescale of healing is important. A respite in diseases such as cancer, might still be regarded as a healing. A 'good' death is a form of healing.
8. The beliefs of the patient are very important in their own right. If they sincerely believe that they have received healing, then this should be respected.
9. What *is* healing? We need to keep this question constantly before us in our assessments. A broad definition might say that God has *in some way* acted in the patient's life. But this can be too nebulous to be useful in any scientific way, and can duck the harder issues. We need to respect the activity of God, whilst increasing the credibility of the church's witness to the healing ministry of Christ. We need to match claim with evidence, and learn from it.
10. The beliefs of the medical profession are highly relevant also. If, *a priori*, the doctors involved are suspicious of the possibility of a physical healing then this is bound to affect the judgements they make (just as do the beliefs of the one healed or the healer). Honest discussion of theological assumptions are part of the assessment procedure.

Where evidence of a physical healing can be substantiated this becomes a strong witness, and potentially has beneficial evangelistic impact upon a very large number of people.

Practical Example: Diocesan Teaching Tour of Eric Delve

Finally, here are two examples of mission settings where the prayer strategy included an expectation of physical healing as *one* possible response by God.

1. In April 1994 the Healing Advisory Group in conjunction with the Council for Evangelism of the Anglican Diocese of Carlisle invited the Revd Eric Delve (from Kirkdale in Liverpool) to undertake a tour of the diocese, teaching on the interrelationship between healing and evangelism. The planning group invited him to 7 different areas of Cumbria. In each area he addressed the overall topic of 'Healing and Evangelism' from a different entry point. The topics were:

- 'Faith for healing'
- 'Healing the heart'
- 'Healing your history'
- 'Building healing into your life'
- 'Healing relationships'
- 'Healing the mind'
- 'Healing through deliverance'

In his preaching Eric Delve aimed to integrate together stories of Christ's healings with the evangelistic potential unleashed by Jesus. As people received Christ's healing so they gave their lives to him in discipleship. Eric urged people to seek healing and respond to the gospel message. It was a powerful combination.

In the evening, at each venue, he spoke at a public meeting (attended by around 200 each night) on aspects of the relationship between healing and evangelism. After he finished speaking opportunity was given for people to come forward to receive prayer for healing. Large numbers of people took up this invitation, revealing many very deep needs. A number of people gave their lives to Christ for the first time, and many others recommitted themselves to Christ. Both of these types of response are part of the evangelistic heart of the gospel.

The following morning at each venue Eric Delve spoke to church leaders, answered questions, and gave opportunity for them to receive prayer with the anointing of oil for service. Some were heartened that he believed in God's power to minister healing through the sacraments too!

The overall effect of this mission was good, in encouraging Christians to ally together healing and evangelism. There were some unchurched who were also touched through the power of this combination approach.

2. During the course of 1994 the churches of the local ecumenical project of Dalton-in-Furness agreed to work together to sponsor the launch of a 'Prayer and Care' scheme across this town of 10,000 people. The scheme is akin to that developed at St.Peter's Conisborough.[21] This scheme is designed to offer Christ's healing love to the townsfolk, without preconditions. There is a long established healing prayer team within the churches, and many members will participate. It will be out of the sensitive offer of prayer for people's healing in various ways that other forms of healing prayer are to be offered. Members of the scheme believe this to be a powerful and appealing combination that will enable the love of Jesus to be released in power through the community, as 'lights in every street'.

---

21 Fully described in Grove Evangelism Booklet 26 *A Prayer-Evanglism Strategy*.

5
Healing Relationships, Including those in the Church

I begin with a quotation from one of the classic writings on holistic healing, from Dr Leslie Weatherhead:

'True spiritual healing demands another kind of preparation altogether. Let a fellowship be formed of convinced, devout and sensible people. Let them regularly pray together. It may be necessary for them to live together for periods. We forget that the disciples lived together (in their mission) for three years, and *lived with Jesus*, and even then were weak and undependable. When all animosities, jealousies, ambitions, prejudices, suspicions and the like have been purged away within the fellowship; when the members of the fellowship have become one, both in flaming love to Christ and in unselfish desire to help others, then they can with confidence claim to be an extension of Christ's body, a part of *"the* church, which *is* his body", and an instrument which the Holy Spirit can use in the ministry of direct spiritual healing.'[22]

I too believe that in the measure that our own relationships (both individually, and corporately within and between churches) are being healed, we shall see the blessing of God come to our churches, and flow out in fruitful mission. At present our generally poor level of relationships hinders the outflow of God's blessing. God will not give fuller blessing until we are more holy vessels for that healing love and grace to flow. And we are often not attractive communities for people to join—we are better known for our problems and divisions!

Churches as Demonstration Models of the Kingdom

The solution lies in our churches becoming demonstration models of the healing love of Christ. Where this healing love is being released others are drawn by its attractiveness to Christ and to his church.

It is vitally important that relationships within our churches are in the process of being healed (as past divisions are either healed through sharing, repentance and forgiveness, or healed through a direct sovereign work of God in prayer), before serious attempts are made in mission. However, the opposite danger should be avoided: waiting until all relationships are healed before active involvement in mission. This can become merely an excuse to put off the 'appointed day' when people have used up their store of excuses to avoid going out to share the gospel.

The church needs to grow as a 'healing community'. As its members experience healing in their relationships, then out of experience and testimony others will be drawn, as the healing church embraces others in God's healing love.

---

22 L Weatherhead, *Psychology, Religion and Healing* (London: Hodders, 1951 edition) p 490.

I was appointed Carlisle Diocesan Healing Adviser whilst Vicar of Coniston and Torver, two small Lake District parishes. It was important for my sense of integrity that I could point to some evidence of God's healing work within these churches. The area where I was able to see the greatest blessing was in the gradual healing of distrustful relationships within the church, between local denominations, and with the community of which these churches were an intrinsic part. It was my experience that as relationships were healed through forgiveness and greater understanding the churches became more effective in their mission and ministry.

The same can be said about the parish where I currently serve as incumbent, in Dalton. One of my principle 'models of ministry' is to be a 'healing reconciler', so that both the tangible relationships and intangible atmosphere of the church can be built up towards a harmonious whole. Newcomers or visitors to our church can sense this, and remark positively upon the greater sense of peace. Out of this credible testimony to Christ's healing, effective mission will become possible, but until then it is all but impossible.

Indeed, I would wish to extend the argument to the whole body of Christ in a prophetic manner. The churches in our nation remain barely committed to serious attempts to heal differences within and between our denominations. Until this is done, the churches of our nation will make little lasting missionary impact. The church, with all its present divisions, needs to repent of attitudes which hinder the witness of Christ to the essential unity of his church. I believe that a focus on the healing power of the gospel can help bring the reconciliation which will give a genuine base for our gospel outreach. In other words, the healing heart of the gospel has the power to bring healing to our churches. The healing movement can actually be a vital means of bringing unity to the whole body of Christ. I have experienced this unifying power whilst receiving Christ's healing at various healing conferences and at 'Houses of Healing' around the country, such as Burrswood, Crowhurst, and Whitehill Chase.

6
Healing in the Wider World: Expressing God's Healing

The scope of healing is broadened out still further in this section. Too often people either conceive of healing in very selfish terms—wanting healing purely to help them feel 'better'—or have a restricted view of healing which keeps it very much within the orbit of the church. I want to contend that since God has a love for all of his world, and is to be found creatively sustaining the whole of his glorious creation, *we* should seek to discover signs of his healing activity throughout the world too, as part of the expression of the incoming kingdom of God. This is prophetically expressed by Jurgen Moltmann:

> 'Miraculous healings were common enough in the ancient world. We find them today too. But in the cause of Jesus they belong within the context of his proclamation of the kingdom of God; when God assumes power over his creation, the demons retreat. When the living God comes and indwells his creation, every creature will be filled with his eternal vitality. Jesus does not bring the kingdom of God only in words that awaken faith; he also brings it in the form of healings which restore health. In the dawn of the new creation of all things, they are not "miracles" at all; they are completely natural and just what we have to expect.'[23]

In the eschatological age of the Spirit, healings are to be expected as part of the normal pattern of life in the kingdom. These words are indeed exciting, challenging, affirming and visionary, from one of the foremost theologians of the twentieth century. They give a cosmic framework for healing in mission.

Having discerned where God is at work in bringing healing, the task of the Christian is to actively cooperate with God in bringing this to completion. This too is the mission of the church, joining as Jesus did with the works of the Father. Effective healing therefore requires sensitivity to the creative Spirit who can be at work in the most surprising situations and people.

There will, on the other hand, be people, places and situations where God's healing work is being actively resisted, and evil destructive powers being released. Healing in this instance requires confrontation, perhaps deliverance, as initial steps in the process of the journey to wholeness.

Practical Outworking

The broader expression of healing as part of the broader mission of the church can occur in many ways:
- Healing of divergent views on the community (that is, in social and political divisions). This extension of Christ's healing power into our communities and

---

[23] J Moltmann, *The Spirit of Life* (London: SCM, 1992) p 190.

wider society is a vital feature of the mission of the church; its social-political activity. For example such healing is desperately needed in Northern Ireland, between racial groups, within poverty- and crime-stricken neighbourhoods, between our social classes in a nation where social and economic divisions are generally acknowledged to be growing, rather than declining. The church, in ministering Christ's healing at this level, has something enormously important, and powerful, to offer.

- Partnership between the church and medical/social service agencies in promoting the welfare of the residents. There are obviously many practical ways of doing this. In Dalton the churches have heavy involvement with *all* the old people's homes in the town. These give opportunity for help at an organisational level, services, pastoral visiting, social events. Focussing on the healing dimension to this involvement stops it becoming simply a form of social work.
- Assisting the 'healing of all creation' through various environmental schemes. Some churches are well placed to give a practical lead in conservation schemes. God's healing and loving energies are always flowing out through Christ's Spirit—the mission of the church is to find practical ways to enable the whole creation to benefit from this healing energy.

7
Practical Ways of Combining Healing and Evangelism

This chapter gives some practical suggestions from my experience. All of these practical ideas can be used, where appropriate, within the mission strategy of an individual or church. We thus use healing as an evangelistic tool with integrity, within the holistic approach advocated in this booklet. There are many others (such as New Age groups) who offer forms of healing as an attractive 'shop window' to their other beliefs through techniques which capture the imagination. Christians can explore various paths, but obviously with Spirit-led discernment.

1. Offer courses in stress management and relaxation into the wider community (a 'bridge' activity which attractively introduces Christ to others). Our parish of Dalton-in-Furness in 1994 invited Mrs Wanda Nash to lead a weekend entitled 'Meeting Christ in Stillness'. It was a very successful weekend, and notably the most popular parts were the sessions of bodily relaxation to soothing words. The weekend had a mission intent, and did attract some people who wouldn't normally attend church. This has been followed by a series of weeknight sessions on relaxing into Christ's love.

2. Use various art forms as therapeutic aids to healing through either evening classes or church projects which others beyond the church community can enter into. There are now many courses at retreat houses around the country which offer such opportunities. Art and craft activities (painting, tapestry, clay, music), with experienced guides, can have enormous therapeutic potential, and attract the unchurched also—thus complementing our mission strategy.
3. Set up a regular clinic sponsored by the church and local medical profession, where people can receive healing care in holistic terms. Such a venture has been mounted in one of the parishes of Carlisle Diocese, Heversham and Milnthorpe. One afternoon a week a local Christian doctor together with the local vicar, his wife, or an experienced member of their congregation have made use of a room in the local doctor's surgery. Local people are making good use of this holistic care and counselling facility.
4. Form a community care forum bringing together all those in an area who are in the 'caring professions'. Such a forum grew up in my previous parish of Coniston. It began as a group who met to talk about ways of helping the elderly of that village. However this grew to become a very useful meeting point to talk over a whole range of issues related to the health of the community. The local doctor and nurses found it an invaluable release for their frustration.
5. Visualise the church's broader mission of social care, and political involvement in terms of *healing*. The same power released in mission to individuals in terms of 'words and works' of the kingdom can come as healing through social care and welfare. Our actions are for the healing of societies' divisions in relationships and structures. An outworking of this in the town of Dalton is the 'Haven' project, which aims to develop a community centre for the use of young people, unemployed and elderly—the most needy and often alienated sections of our community. This partnership between the churches, town council and other caring agencies is regarded by us as an important practical expression of our own and Christ's healing work within the town's communities.
6. Start environmental care projects which extend beyond the care of the churchyard! I know of a church that has in its grounds a small garden of peace for prayer and meditation. Many church grounds have space to establish havens of peace and tranquillity where people can pause to meet Christ within his creation, receiving healing to body, mind and spirit as they rest and pray.
7. Use healing services evangelistically, advertising both the breadth of healing potentially available, and that no guarantees of cure are offered. A survey conducted in Carlisle Diocese in 1992 revealed that some 15-20% of parishes offered prayers for healing, either within a main service such as Holy Communion, or (more rarely) as a separate special service. Generally these special healing services brought in the committed faithful Christians, with few newcomers. I believe that greater attempts could and should be made to offer these more widely, with plenty of unashamed publicity, to the unchurched, as a major part of a church's mission strategy. The general public responds well to visits by faith healers; I see no reason why we should not, with responsibil-

ity, build upon this obvious need. There is great scope for imagination in a form of service that can be used in various settings: festival of health, annual service with medical professionals, meditation, celebration of life in fullness.[24]

8. Regular and enthusiastic use of the sacraments, perhaps with a more open and embracing policy than is often considered. It is my conviction that all the sacraments can be agencies of healing when so understood, most notably of course Holy Communion and anointing with oil. It has been my experience that when teaching is given on the healing power of the sacraments (including baptism and marriage) the grace of Christ and his presence is received in new and beautiful ways into people's lives. The teaching of Leanne Payne on experiencing the healing presence of Christ through the sacraments is of particular value here. At a recent conference which I attended one of the most powerful moments occurred as we asked God to heal our spirits through the cleansing power of forgiveness. As we received God's forgiveness 'holy water' was sprinkled liberally upon us by members of her prayer team![25]

9. Build a pastoral care and outreach team who can minister the love of Christ through word and action. Such a team is being developed at Dalton-in-Furness, within the Local Ecumenical Project. We have even managed to gain the full cooperative support of the town council! See the explanation given in chapter 4. As these are released into the town we expect considerable response to Jesus' way of mission, meeting a range of personal needs out in the 'marketplace' of people's homes and other buildings outside the church building., where God's compassionate power will be greatest.

10. Hospital and hospice ministry provides another excellent opportunity. This should not be left to the clergy alone! Our church in Dalton joins a rota with other local churches to visit our local hospital, and help in services in the chapel. A church I attended as a teenager held their own ward services every Sunday afternoon. Church members can be encouraged to visit hospital or hospice to visit church members and neighbours, ending their visit with a prayer.

Bishop John Finney has made a plea for healing to be primarily a ministry exercised outside of the church building. His justification comes direct from Jesus' approach. Healing was directed outwards, and never during Jesus' life inwards towards the disciples themselves. The above suggestions would help to fulfil the request by Finney during the Decade of Evangelism. He is very positive in his belief in the power of such an alliance, however; 'In the New Testament the ministry of healing was predominantly an *evangelistic* ministry'.[26] John Wimber talks in terms of 'power evangelism' and 'power healing'. In both instances the theory and practice of Vineyard churches is to move out amongst the unchurched to minister healing and evangelism in the power of the kingdom.[27]

---

24 See an excellent selection of prayers, readings and orders of service in H Booth, *Seven Whole Days* (London: Arthur James, 1992).
25 The conference was in September 1994, at Swanwick, sponsored by 'Pastoral Care Ministries'. See also J McManus, *The Healing Power of the Sacraments* (Notre Dame: Ave Maria, 1984).
26 *Healing and Wholeness* magazine, July 1991.
27 See J Wimber, *Power Healing* (London: Hodders, 1986).

8
Conclusion

George Bennett, one of pioneers of the healing ministry in this century, writes:
'The rediscovery by the church of her healing ministry seems to find its significance when seen as an integral part of the unfolding of God's plan for his creation and especially for his church. For though we say we are rediscovering our healing ministry, it is more true to say that it is the Holy Spirit who is restoring it. In other words this is a phenomenon *that is happening to us*. You and I are caught up in it. And not only we but also our fellow-Christians throughout the world are being touched by this same movement of the Spirit in our days.[28]

These prophetic words are even more true today than they were in 1979. Many involved in the work of healing feel that they are being 'caught up' in a movement of God that is irresistible, not for the church alone but for the whole of God's world in these days of unparalleled crisis yet opportunity. Morton Kelsey convincingly shows that the healing ministry has never been 'lost' to the church, but has been especially rediscovered today. He argues that the healing power of the 'good news' can affect every area of human existence, but above all within the human soul. As we have considered the ways in which this healing power of Christ's Spirit can bring wholeness, health, reconciliation and salvation, we have seen its great potential for strengthening the mission of the church.[29]

It is not a question of rivalry between the preaching and healing ministries, but should be seen as a *partnership*. It is a synergistic working together of healing and evangelism in the good news of the kingdom that Christ came to announce and usher in. Different gifts lie within the body of Christ, and as Paul explains in 1 Corinthians 12 (where he opens the possibility of a range of different ministries of healing-specialisms), the church requires them all for its witness. The current greatest need within the church is for its members to be helped to discover these gifts and released into exercising them for the advancement of the kingdom of God.

---

[28] G Bennett, *Commissioned to Heal* (Evesham: Arthur James, 1979 edition) p 58.
[29] M Kelsey, *Healing and Christianity* (New York: Harper & Row, 1973).